Disgusting Body Facts

Twitches and Sneezes

Angela Royston

www.raintreepublishers.co.uk
Visit our website to find out
more information about
Raintree books.

To ord
☎ Phor
🖹 Fax –
🖵 Visit

Edited by Nancy Dickmann, Sian Smith, and
  Rebecca Rissman
Designed by Joanna Hinton Malivoire
Original illustrations ©Capstone Global Library 2010
Original illustrations by Christian Slade
Picture research by Tracy Cummins
Originated by Capstone Global Library Ltd
Printed and bound in China by Leo Paper Products Ltd

ISBN 978 1 4062 1304 1 (hardback)
14 13 12 11 10
10 9 8 7 6 5 4 3 2 1

British Library Cataloguing in Publication Data
Royston, Angela.
  Twitches and sneezes. -- (Disgusting body facts)
  1. Sneezing--Juvenile literature. 2. Spasms--Juvenile
  literature. 3. Symptoms--Juvenile literature.
  I. Title II. Series
  616'.047-dc22

Acknowledgements
We would like to thank the following for permission to
reproduce photographs:
Alamy p. **10** (©Christina Kennedy); Getty Images
pp. **8** (©Niklas Thiemann), **11** (©Donn Thompson),
12 (©Simon Songhurst), **19** (©3D4Medical.com),
26 (©Bernhard Lang), **29** (©3D Clinic); Photo
Researchers, Inc. pp. **21** (©E. Gray), **25** (©Scimat);
Photolibrary pp. **15** (©Stockbyte), **17** (©Custom
Medical Stock Photo), **22** (©Spike Mafford); Phototake
p. **7** (©Collection CNRI); Shutterstock pp. **19 bottom**
(©Oberon), **27** (©Robert Gubbins).

Cover photograph of a man sneezing reproduced with
permission of Getty Images (©Peter Cade).

Every effort has been made to contact copyright
holders of material reproduced in this book. Any
omissions will be rectified in subsequent printings if
notice is given to the publishers.

All the Internet addresses (URLs) given in this book
were valid at the time of going to press. However, due
to the dynamic nature of the Internet, some addresses
may have changed, or sites may have changed or
ceased to exist since publication. While the author and
publishers regret any inconvenience this may cause
readers, no responsibility for any such changes can be
accepted by either the author or the publishers.

Some words are shown in bold, **like this.** You can find
out what they mean by looking in the glossary.

Contents

No control

You can't help twitching and sneezing. Your body does this whether you like it or not!

Did you know?

You sneeze and cough when your body wants to get rid of dust, **germs** that can make you ill, and other unwanted things. However, you can sometimes hiccup for no reason at all!

5

Hic!

Hiccups are caused by the large, flat **muscle** that makes you breathe in. This muscle is just below your **lungs**. Sometimes it twitches. This makes you take in a sudden breath of air.

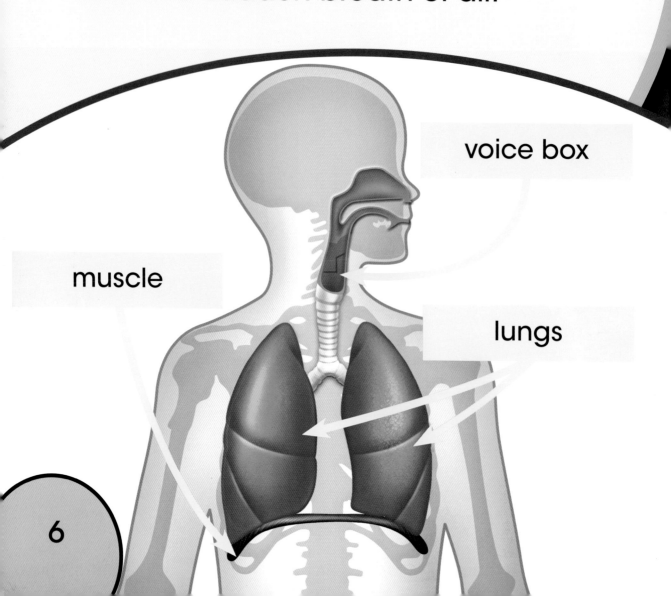

voice box

muscle

lungs

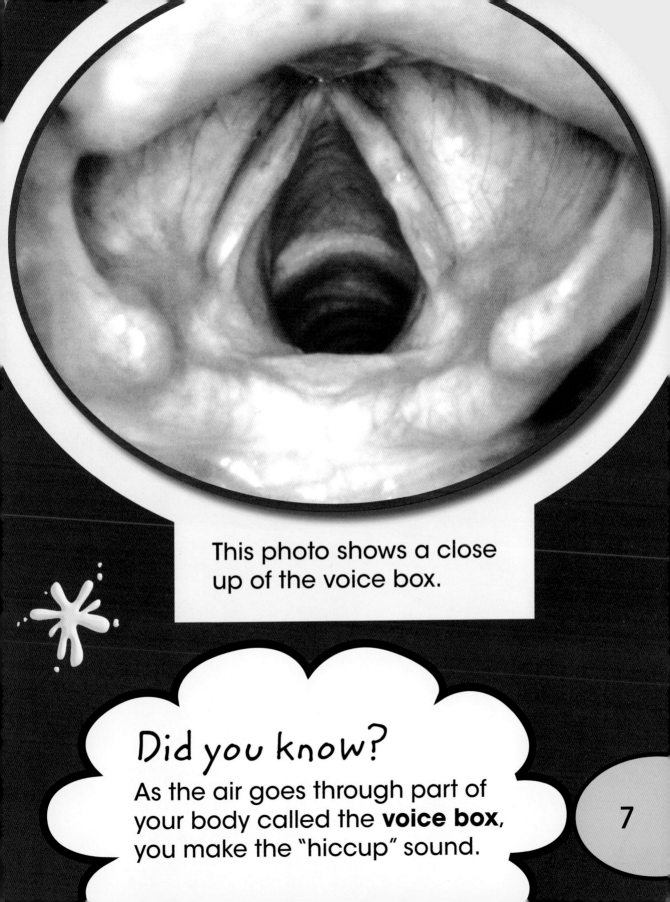

This photo shows a close up of the voice box.

Did you know?

As the air goes through part of your body called the **voice box**, you make the "hiccup" sound.

What causes hiccups?

These things often make you hiccup:

- gobbling your food too fast
- laughing and drinking at the same time
- eating very fresh bread.

But sometimes you hiccup for no reason!

Did you know?

Charles Osborne, from Iowa in the United States, had the longest attack of hiccups ever. They lasted for 68 years!

9

Hiccup cures

Different cures for hiccups work for different people. These are some hiccup cures:

- hold your breath
- drink from the wrong side of the cup
- eat a teaspoon of sugar
- stick out your tongue and yawn.

Did you know?

Many hiccup cures work by getting the person with hiccups to relax or by distracting them. This means getting them to think about something else.

11

Blinking

If an insect or speck of dust comes near your eye, you blink without thinking. Sometimes you do not blink fast enough and a fly goes into your eye!

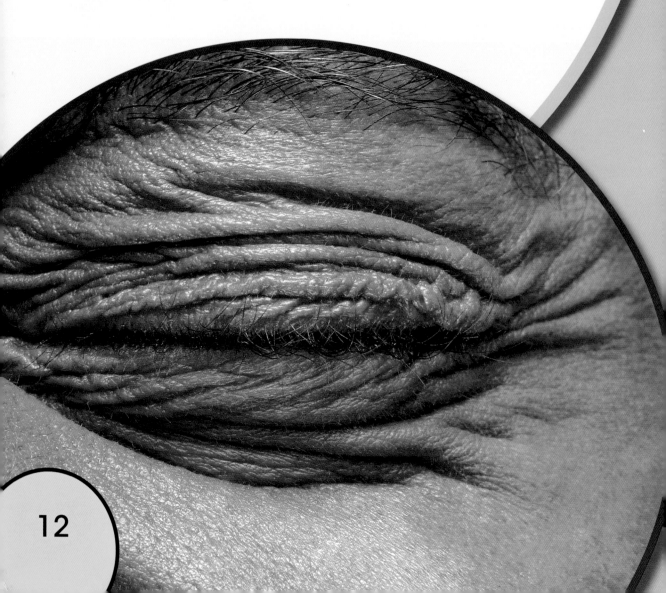

Did you know?

Most people blink about once every four seconds. You probably blink about 21,600 times every day!

13

Choking

Food goes down your throat into a tube to your stomach. Air goes down your throat, too. It goes down a different tube to your **lungs**. Your lungs are parts of your body you use to breathe.

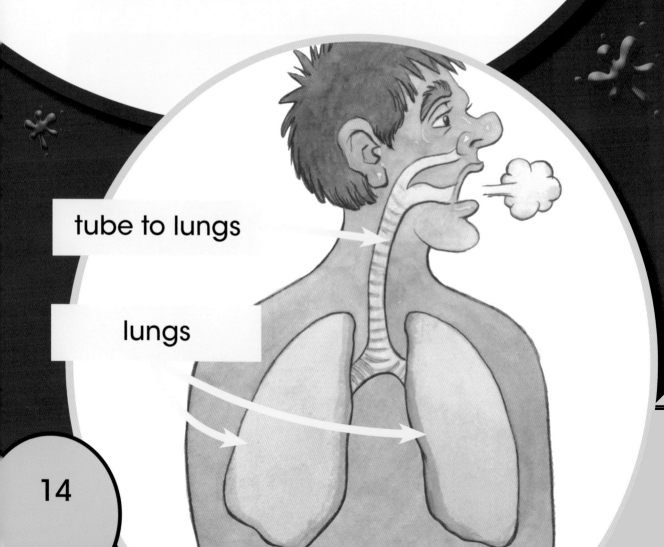

tube to lungs

lungs

Sometimes a bit of food goes down the wrong tube. Then you cough and choke until the food comes back into your mouth.

15

A-A-Atishoo!

You sneeze when something tickles the inside of your nose. Sneezing forces air out of your **lungs**. **Mucus**, or snot, shoots out of your nose. With luck, the mucus washes out whatever is tickling your nose.

Did you know?

When you sneeze, air blasts through your nose at over 93 miles per hour (150 kilometres per hour). This is faster than a car on the motorway!

17

Sign of a cold?

The air you breathe often contains dust and other things. Most things are too small to see, but they can tickle your nose. They include tiny living things called cold **germs**. Sneezing shows you could be getting a cold.

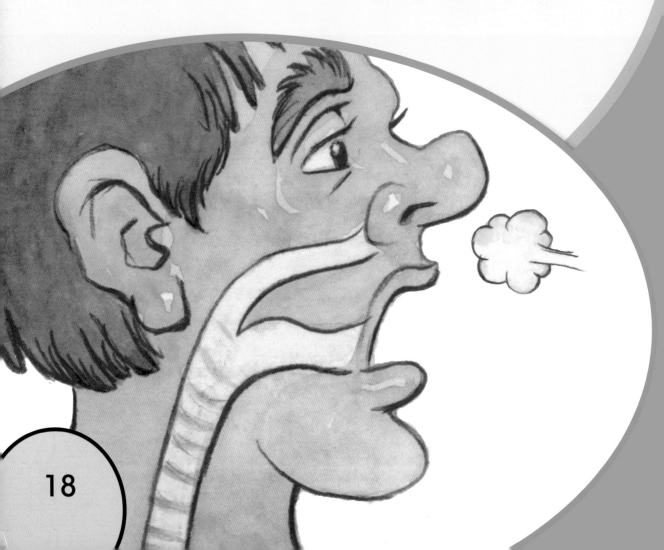

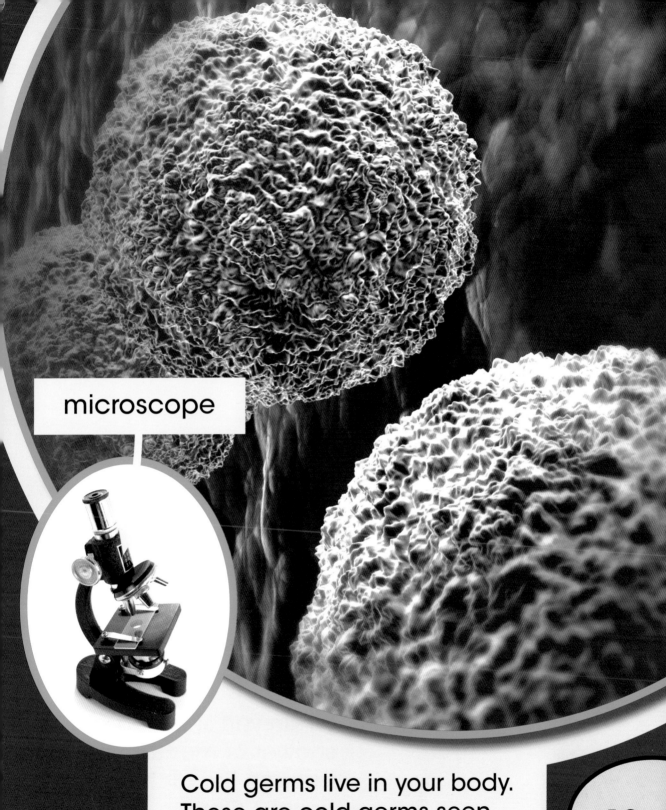

microscope

Cold germs live in your body. These are cold germs seen through a microscope.

Hay fever

The air you breathe often contains **pollen**. Pollen is the powder you can find in flowers. Some people are **allergic** to pollen. This means that their bodies react badly to it. They sneeze, their eyes itch, and their noses run. This is called **hay fever**.

Did you know?

When you sneeze, a shower of **mucus** blasts through the air. It can travel 3.5 metres. It can go from one end of a room to the other!

This is the inside of someone's throat seen under a microscope. The bits of pollen trapped there have been coloured in pink.

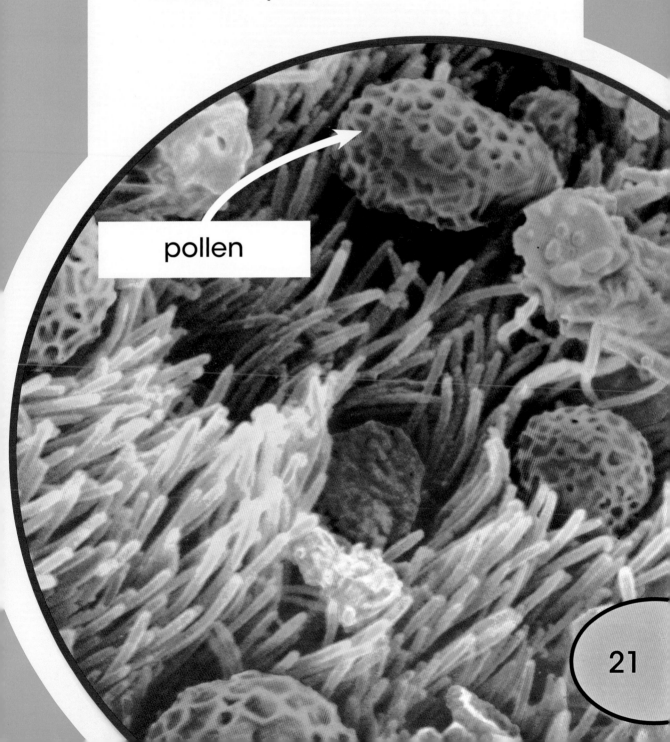

pollen

Sniffing and blowing

Sometimes your nose fills up with **mucus**, or snot. Sniffing pulls the mucus back into your nose.

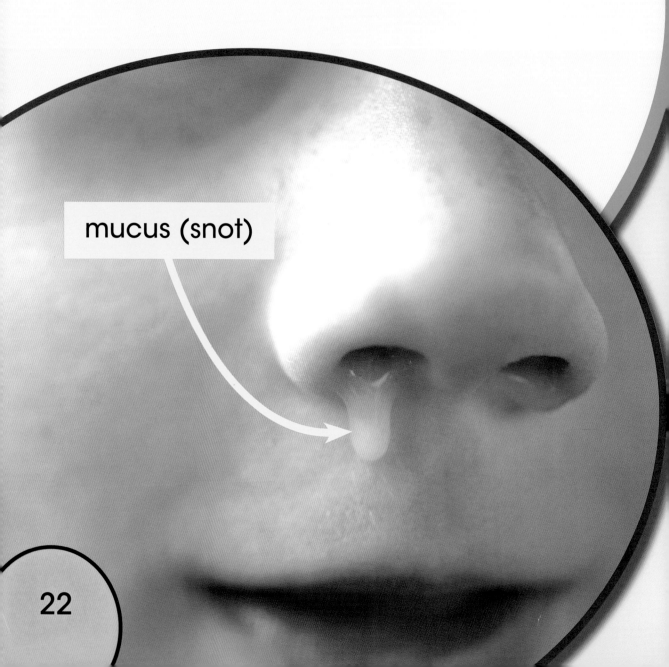

mucus (snot)

tissue

You blow your nose when you want to get rid of snot. Make sure you have a tissue ready to catch the snot!

23

Coughs

Coughing forces air out of your **lungs** into your mouth. The air helps to clear **mucus** from your lungs. As you cough, tiny drops of spit spray into the air!

mucus

Did you know?

When you are healthy you still have a lot of different types of **germs** living in your mouth. When you have a cold, your spit contains millions of extra germs.

Catch the germs!

Sneezing and coughing spread cold and flu **germs**. Do not pass your germs on to other people. Catch them in a paper tissue and throw them in the bin.

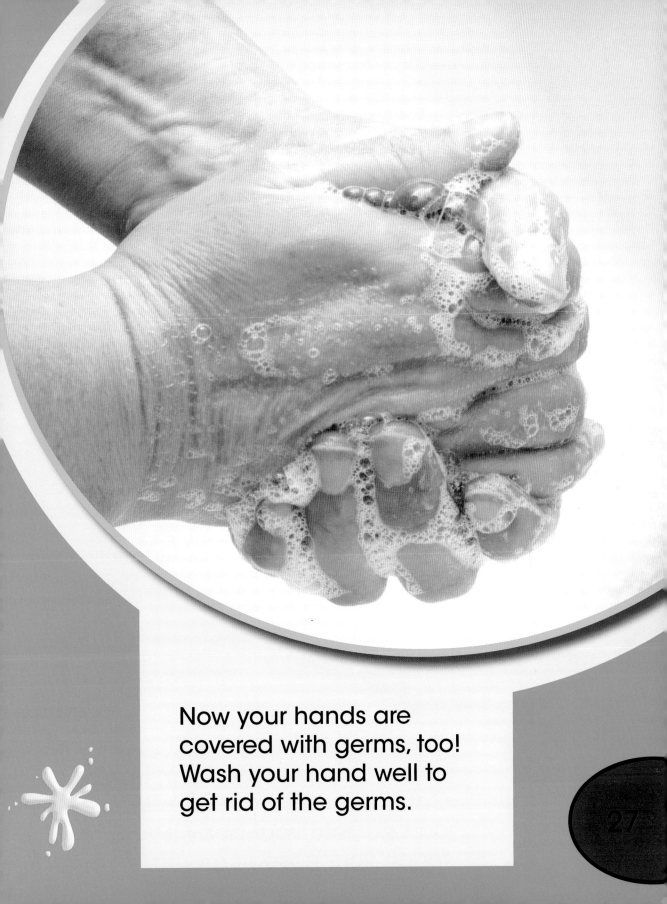

Now your hands are
covered with germs, too!
Wash your hand well to
get rid of the germs.

More about breathing and colds

You catch a cold when cold **germs** get inside your nose and throat.

The tube that goes from your throat to your **lungs** looks like a vacuum cleaner hose! It is called the **trachea**.

An adult's lungs hold about 5 litres of air. A child's lungs could hold about 3 litres of air.

1 litre is about the same as 4 glasses.

Cold germs can get into your body if you breathe them in. Cold germs on your hands can get into your body if you touch your nose or mouth.

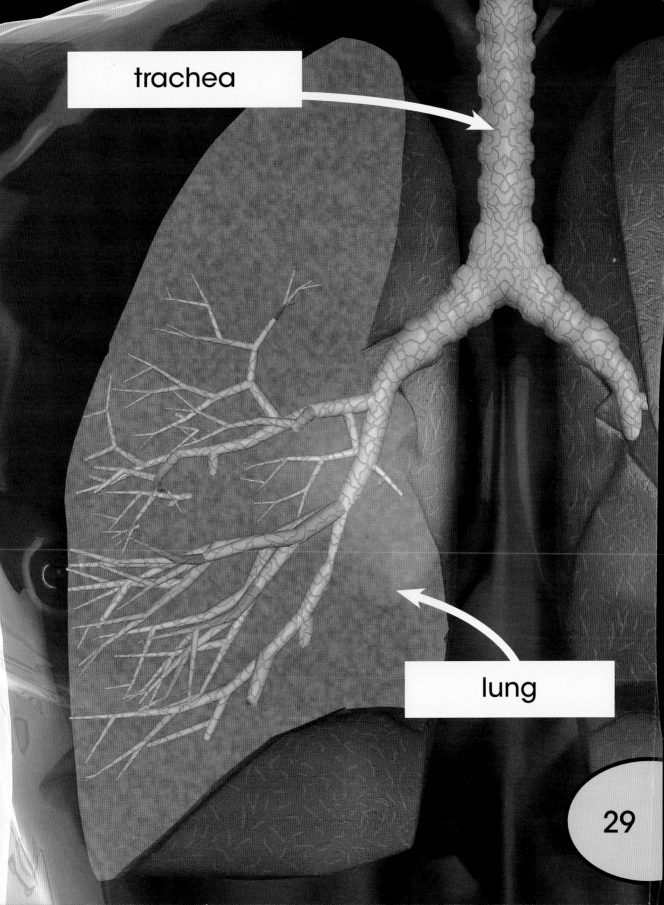

trachea

lung

Glossary

allergic very sensitive to something. When you are allergic to something your body reacts badly to it.

germs tiny living things that can make you ill if they get inside your body

hay fever if people are allergic to pollen they might get hay fever. Hay fever makes you sneeze and gives you itchy eyes and a runny nose.

lungs parts of your body where air goes when you breathe in. You have two lungs in your chest.

mucus slimy liquid that lines tubes and other parts inside your body

muscles parts of your body that you use to move your bones, lungs, and other parts of your body

pollen powder made by flowers

trachea tube that goes from your throat to your lungs

voice box special part of the throat which you use to make sounds

Find out more

Find out

How much snot can your body make when you have a cold?

Books

How's Your Health? Colds and Flu, Angela Royston (Franklin Watts, 2006)

My Amazing Body: Breathing, Angela Royston (Raintree, 2004)

My Best Book of the Human Body, Barbara Taylor (Kingfisher Books, 2008)

Websites

kids.aol.co.uk/slimey-facts-about-snot/article/20080707101809990001
This fun website is full of interesting facts about mucus or snot.

kidshealth.org/kid/htbw/htbw_main_page.html
This website tells you how different parts of the body work. Click on "lungs" as it comes along to see how they work. Click on "nose" and find out more about sneezing.

www.hygiene-educ.com/en/home.htm
This fun website has games and information about germs and how to avoid them.

Index